THE PRESIDENCY

The Presidency

Carl R. Green, Ph.D., and William R. Sanford, Ph.D.

The Rourke Corporation, Inc.

The Rourke Corporation, Inc.
P.O. Box 3328, Vero Beach, FL 32964

Green, Carl R.
    The presidency / by Carl R. Green and William R. Sanford.
        p.   cm. — (American government)
        Summary: Describes the duties, responsibilities, and powers of president of the
    United States.
        ISBN 0-86593-084-8
        1. Presidents—United States—Juvenile literature.
    [1. Presidents.]   I. Sanford, William R. (William Reynolds), 1927-.
    II. Title.   III. Series.
    JK517.G74   1990   90-8639
    353.03'13—dc20   CIP
                                                                         AC

Series Editor: Gregory Lee
Editors: Elizabeth Sirimarco, Marguerite Aronowitz
Book design and production: The Creative Spark,
  Capistrano Beach, CA
Cover photograph: AP/Wide World Photos, Inc.

Authors' Note

All descriptions of the workings of the American Government that appear in this book are authentic, as are the citations of historical figures and events. Only the characters who carry the story line are fictional—and we have modeled them as closely as possible upon their real-life counterparts.

Table of Contents

1

Welcome To The White House

The note was waiting on Karen Rossi's desk when she returned from lunch. She saw the printed heading and swallowed hard. What did Chief of Staff Billings want with her? The brief message read, "See me as soon as you come in." It was signed, "Chet."

Was she in some kind of trouble? She'd only been working in the Executive Office of the White House for two weeks. Like most of the other summer interns, she was still waiting to be given a real job. The White House staff moved at a fast trot, leaving the interns to catch on as best they could.

Karen headed for the chief of staff's office in the West Wing. Except for a brief tour when she arrived, she'd never been this close to the Oval Office before. The president was out of town today, so the corridors were quiet.

After passing several uniformed guards, Karen was shown into the chief of staff's office. Chet Billings was talking to a young woman of about 22, Karen's own age. Reporters called Chet the "power behind the Oval Office." As chief of staff, he was involved in everything the president did. The smile he gave Karen reassured her. She wasn't in trouble after all.

George Washington, our first president, firmly resisted one idea: that he—or any future president—become the king of the United States of America.

"Ms. Rossi," Billings said, "this is Marisa Parador, the daughter of one of the South American ambassadors. Her father was a college classmate of mine." His voice sharpened as he looked at his watch. "Please give Marisa an insider's tour while her father is meeting with the national security advisor. I'm late for a meeting or I'd do it myself."

A few minutes later, Karen and Marisa were on their way. The pass that Billings gave them allowed them to peek into the Oval Office. Karen pointed to the handsome wooden desk. "This is where our President works," she whispered.

Marisa nodded her approval. "Yes, this is a proper office for the person your country elects as its leader," she said. "My own country is once again electing its president. Not long ago, we were ruled by generals who cared nothing for democracy."

Karen searched her memory. She remembered that Washington, Jackson, Grant and Eisenhower were generals before they became president. But none of them had tried to hold the office by force when their terms ended. More often they were lawyers who went on to become state governors or members of Congress before running for the White House. But that was only a custom, not a requirement, she recalled.

Each bit of information seemed to trigger a new question. Karen led her guest back to her own office. "We might as well be comfortable while we talk," she thought.

The Two-Term Limit

"Now, tell me," Marisa said as she sipped a cup of coffee. "Is it true that anyone can become president of this country?"

"The Constitution lists just three requirements," Karen explained. "A candidate must be 35 years old, a native-born citizen, and a resident of the U.S. for at least 14 years. Beyond that, political realities take over. Candidates need the support of one of the two major political parties. It also helps if they come from a big state with lots of voters, look good on television, can speak well, and inspire the voters with confidence in their abilities."

What Does The President Say At The Inauguration?

Ronald Reagan took the inaugural oath for his second term as president on January 21, 1985. As he laid his hand on the Bible held by Chief Justice Warren Burger, he repeated the same Oath of Office used by 39 predecessors. The oath comes directly from the United States Constitution:

"I do solemnly swear that I will faithfully execute the office of President of the United States, and will to the best of my ability, preserve, protect, and defend the Constitution of the United States."

With those few words, the president assumes office. From that moment on, he (and someday, she) possesses all the privileges and challenges that go with the position. Moments after being sworn in, the president delivers his inaugural address. The words that President Reagan delivered on that occasion are typical of these talks to the American people.

Reagan said, "There are no words adequate to express my thanks for the great honor that you've bestowed on me. I will do my utmost to be deserving of your trust.

"This is...the fiftieth time that we, the people, have celebrated this historic occasion. When the first president, George Washington, placed his hand upon the Bible, he stood less than a single day's journey by horseback from raw, untamed wilderness. There were four million Americans in a Union of 13 states.

"Today we are 60 times as many in a Union of 50 states. We've lighted the world with our inventions, gone to the aid of mankind wherever in the world there was a cry for help, journeyed to the moon and safely returned.

"So much has changed. And yet we stand together as we did two centuries ago.

"When I took this oath four years ago, I did so in a time of economic stress. Voices were raised saying that we had to look to our past for the greatness and glory. But we, the present-day Americans, are not given to looking backward. In this blessed land, there is always a better tomorrow."

The Oval Office. The president meets daily with ʈ

...isors and receives visitors to the White House here.

Marisa knew that some of her country's presidents held on to power for many years. In some cases, it had taken a revolution to remove them from office. "What limits do you place on the time your presidents stay in office?" she asked.

Karen replied that presidents are elected to four-year terms. If they want a second term, they must run again. As the nation's first president, George Washington set a tradition of serving only two terms. He thought that allowing more than eight years of rule by one person might lead to a dictatorship.

"Your Franklin Roosevelt was elected four times," Marisa protested.

"Roosevelt ran for a third term in 1940 because he knew the country would soon be at war," Karen said. "Then, in 1944, with World War II still dragging on, he was elected a fourth time. He died in 1945, soon after he started his fourth term."

"Could your current president run for a third term?"

Karen shook her head. Since 1951, the 22nd Amendment has limited presidents to two terms. Only a vice president who becomes president because of the death or resignation of the former president can serve longer. If a vice president inherits a term of less than two years, he or she can be elected to two additional terms. Thus, no president can serve longer than nine years and 364 days.

Some experts believe the two-term amendment is unwise. Because of it, the nation might have to elect a new and untested leader during a war. But amending the Constitution isn't easy. First, Congress must pass the new amendment. Then the legislatures of 38 states must approve it. In 200 years, only 26 amendments have made it that far.

"Limiting the time a president can remain in office is a good idea," Marisa said. "Your people will never have to start a revolution to force someone out of the White House."

Replacing A President

Marisa picked up Karen's copy of the United States Constitution. The presidency took up only four sections, two of them

The presidency is really seven jobs in one. Some presidents emphasize one or two of the jobs over the others, but no successful president can ignore any of them. The seven jobs, along with a brief description of the duties that go with each one, are as follows:

Chief of State:
Performs ceremonial duties
Stands as symbol of the United States

Chief Executive:
Administers federal programs and budgets
Supervises federal employees
"Sells" programs to public

Commander-In-Chief:
Decides on military policies and strategy
Guards the national security
Maintains civilian control of the armed forces

Chief Politician:
Leads party, supports its candidates
Helps influence party platform

Chief Diplomat:
Establishes foreign policy and writes its treaties
Carries on diplomatic relations with foreign countries

Chief Legislator:
Proposes legislation to Congress
Urges passage of needed bills
Reports to Congress on the State of the Union

Chief of State:
Enforces court decisions
Appoints federal judiciary
Uses right of pardon

*While the White House is the official residence of the president
and the president's family, its place in American history
makes it one of the most popular tourist attractions
in Washington, D.C.*

quite short. "You are lucky to live in a country that respects its basic law," she said. "In Latin America, we also have fine constitutions. But our generals and politicians sometimes ignore them."

Karen remembered the president's inauguration two years ago. Even though the hard-fought campaign had left many people angry, no one challenged the outcome. Now the losers were making plans to try to win the next election.

Marisa had another thought. "It's dangerous for countries that don't have a democratic history to have a leader die in office," she commented. "We must hope the generals will accept our new civilian president."

"There's no danger of a military takeover here," Karen replied. "William Harrison, our ninth president, was in office less than a month before he died. Since then, three presidents have been shot to death, four more died of illness, and one resigned. In each case, the vice president took over, just as the Constitution provides."

Karen remembered that one vice president had referred to the office as "not worth a bucket of warm spit." The only constitutional duty given to vice presidents is to preside over the Senate. In practice, they show up only when they're needed to cast a tie-breaking vote. Modern-day vice presidents keep busy by heading commissions, attending Cabinet meetings, and making goodwill visits. They have little real power—until the moment they're called to step into the presidency.

"What if a president becomes seriously ill?" Marisa asked.

"The Constitution allows the V.P. to take over for a disabled president," Karen said. "But it doesn't define disability. Until 1967 the country had to wait for a disabled president to recover, die, or be replaced at the next election. The problem was solved by the 25th Amendment, which spells out the procedure for replacing a disabled president. The amendment also allows the president to return to office after the disability ends."

"You said that one of your presidents resigned his office," Marisa said. "Why would anyone do that?"

Karen explained that Richard Nixon had resigned rather than face an impeachment trial in the Senate. To complicate matters, Vice

President Spiro Agnew had resigned a year earlier and Congressman Gerald Ford had replaced him. Thus, Nixon's resignation turned the presidency over to Ford. For the only time in American history, the country was led by someone who had not been elected as president or vice president.

A Well-Kept House

The two young women chatted quietly as they walked through the ground floor rooms of the White House. Marisa asked to see the president's living quarters. Karen told her that the family's second floor rooms were private.

"This is really my second tour," Marisa confessed. "I waited in line this morning with the other tourists and a guide took us through the public rooms." She touched a fine antique chair. "It's wonderful that the White House is open to the public."

Karen thought so, too. She sometimes wondered what it had been like back in 1800 when John and Abigail Adams first moved in. Until this century people had often walked in off the street with every expectation of seeing the president. Over the years the White House had been remodeled and become more formal. Today, it serves as historic site, presidential home, and presidential office. Visitors are allowed to tour only the finely furnished public rooms on the first floor. The first family occupies the second floor living quarters, and the east and west wings house the executive office staff.

"I saw the Cabinet room just after we left the Oval Office," Marisa said. "What other offices are in the west wing?"

"The White House has its own pecking order," Karen said. "Your importance is judged by how close your office is to the president. You saw that Mr. Billings works just around the corner from the Oval Office, so he's pretty important. The vice president has an office nearby, and so do the other top aides. And I'm in the basement," she laughed. "Actually, I could be further away," she continued. "Many staffers work in the Old Executive Office Building next door, and the Cabinet departments have offices all over Washington."

Marisa was impressed by the spotless appearance of the White House. Karen told her that one worker does nothing but wash windows and clean chandeliers. Some of the crystal chandeliers take 14 hours to polish. Other workers wax the floors every day, and vacuum the heavily used carpets as often as six times a day. The chefs are always ready to prepare lunch for four or a banquet of 400.

Just then a guard approached to tell them that Marisa's father was waiting. Karen led the way to the front portico. She received a warm hug from her new friend before Marisa climbed into a long black sedan.

"That was an unusual afternoon's work," Karen thought as she walked back to her office. "I wonder what tomorrow will bring."

2

The President As Chief Executive

At ten o'clock the next morning Karen Rossi was called to Chet Billings' office once again. The Chief of Staff was alone this time. "Dr. Parador called to express his thanks for the tour you arranged yesterday," he said. "It sounds as though you gave Marisa a good lecture on the presidency."

Karen felt herself blush. Had she said something wrong? No, Billings was smiling.

"Look," he said, "how would you like to work for me this summer? Before you answer, I should tell you that this office works long hours. We average a crisis a day around here."

"When I applied for this internship I knew it wouldn't be a vacation," Karen responded. "I want to learn as much as I can before I go back to college in the fall."

Billings picked up a folder. "Prepare a handout on 'The Seven Jobs of the President'," he said. "Give me something that answers visitors' questions before they ask them."

Karen didn't hesitate. "When do I start?" she asked.

"You just did," Billings said with a chuckle, handing her a typed outline.

Karen studied the outline. Billings had given her a week. That meant she'd have to complete one job a day. The first job on the list

*Camp David is a presidential retreat in the mountains of Maryland,
allowing the chief executive and family to escape from
the daily pressures of Washington.*

read, "The President as Chief Executive." The Chief Executive's role,
she knew, was like that of the head of an enormous corporation. In this
case the "corporation" was the entire executive branch of the United
States government.

Like any top-level executive, the president has to make decisions
about policy. For example, should more money be spent on Head Start
programs? If the answer is "yes" and Congress agrees, more decisions
have to be made. How will the money be handed out? How can the
government be sure the money is well spent? The president has to stay
on top of this and a thousand other administrative details.

No one expects the president to do it all himself. Day-to- day management is delegated to the members of the Cabinet and various federal agencies. Each secretary is responsible for a major area of national life—Agriculture, Defense, Education, Labor, Energy, and so on. Picking the right people for the top jobs begins right after a president wins the November election.

Some department heads are chosen because they're political allies or personal friends. Others earn their posts because they've shown their ability in other jobs. After the President takes office, the names of the nominees go to the Senate for approval. Almost all are approved.

To a large degree, Karen realized, the Chief Executive is judged by the success of his appointments. When agency heads do good work, the president looks good. But when they fail and scandal strikes, the president must shoulder much of the blame. After all, he's the one who appointed them.

Never Embarrass The Chief

After a quick lunch in the White House cafeteria, Karen talked to the president's personal secretary. She looked like a kindly grandmother, but Fran Halligan was a tough, experienced woman and fiercely loyal to "the Chief."

"The Cabinet is important," Halligan told Karen, "but modern presidents rely on their aides. That's why the White House staff has grown in recent years. The Chief appoints his staff without the fuss of winning the Senate's approval."

Karen learned that the president's top aides influence policy in many ways. They draw up schedules and budgets, plan trips, and write speeches. To a great extent, the Chief of Staff even controls access to the president. "A weak president," she thought, "might find it easy to let his staff run the country in his name."

Halligan described the selection process. First, very few aides have held political office. Most staffers are long-time friends and political allies of the president. Others are professors, lawyers, or corporate executives. Whatever their background, aides must be loyal. If

*Rose garden ceremonies at the White House are a regular
part of the president's duties as the chief executive.*

two Cabinet secretaries disagree, the staff's job is to clarify their differences. Then the president can choose between the opposing points of view.

"I read recently that aides sometimes make decisions in the president's name," Karen said.

The charge didn't ruffle Halligan. "The Chief must delegate authority," she explained. "If he's dealing with nuclear disarmament, he doesn't always have time to meet with the British prime minister. Problems can develop when aides keep important information from the president. They may think they know what's best, or they may be trying to help him avoid a political trap.

"An aide once tried to defeat the new gas tax bill by telling the press that a veto was certain, when, in fact, the president hadn't yet made up his mind. That young man is no longer with us."

Karen understood. The staff makes it possible for the Chief

What Does The President Do In A Typical Day?

From the time he wakes up until he goes to bed at night, almost every minute of the president's day is scheduled for him. No two days are ever alike, but a typical day at the White House looks something like this.

Time	Activity
6:30 A.M.	Wake-up call comes from White House switchboard. President skims morning newspapers and watches television news. Breakfasts with First Lady.
7:40	Chief of staff briefs president on day's schedule. National security advisor arrives to discuss CIA report that a Middle Eastern country is making chemical weapons.
8:15	President walks to Oval Office to begin day's work. Reads daily news digest prepared by aides.
8:50	Press secretary delivers draft of speech president will give at United Nations. President edits the speech and takes advantage of quiet time to catch up on paperwork.
10:00	President convenes meeting of his Cabinet. Discussion centers on budget problems.
11:05	Television crew arrives. President uses interview to appeal to the public for support of new trade treaty.
11:30	New ambassador from Poland presents his credentials. President confers with him on economic aid package.

12:05 P.M.	Congressional leaders arrive for working lunch. They report to president on progress of bills he wants passed.
1:00	President returns to his bedroom to shower, change clothes, and relax for 30 minutes.
1:50	President returns to Oval Office to meet with secretary of state and vice president. They discuss vice president's coming trip to Latin America.
2:35	Press secretary arrives to rehearse president for press conference. First lady stops by to confer with the president about her anti-smoking campaign.
3:00	President holds press conference, speaks on budget plans and answers questions on various topics.
3:40	Aides arrange Rose Garden ceremony to honor Eagle Scouts. President presents awards and speaks on his own experiences as a Boy Scout.
3:55	President returns to Oval Office to sign papers that require his signature.
4:30	Attorney General arrives to discuss anti-drug program.
5:15	President goes to East Room for reception honoring new members of Congress.
5:55	President returns to family quarters for quiet dinner with first lady and visiting family members.
8:00	Secret Service escorts President to Washington hotel where he speaks to Association of Senior Citizens.
9:20	President returns to White House. Winds down by watching an old movie. Lights out at 11:40.

Executive to do his job, but individual members are expendable. Whether they work near the Oval Office or in a basement cubbyhole, they must never embarrass the Chief. They may be the brains behind a new policy, but the president gets the credit. They can twist the arm of a Cabinet member or bully a Pentagon admiral, but the public must never know. From the outside, it should look as though the Chief Executive is completely in charge.

The OMB

A Chief Executive needs money to run the government, and money means budgets. "How does the Chief Executive decide on the federal budget?" Karen wondered. That question sent her to the Executive Office Building to visit the Office of Management and Budget, or OMB.

Five minutes later she was sitting in the office of Morgan Best, the O.M.B.'s assistant director for public affairs. "Is this where the budget gets put together?" she asked.

Morgan nodded. He explained that O.M.B.'s computers work all year to come up with some educated guesses. The agency estimates how much money the government will take in and how much it will spend. The revenues come mostly from personal and corporate income taxes. The expenditures pay for everything from missiles to mousetraps.

He held up a computer printout covered with columns of numbers. "That's the budget request from the Department of Housing and Urban Development," he said. "In a few days we'll be meeting with the H.U.D. secretary to talk about these numbers."

"Will H.U.D. get everything it's asking for? I know how badly the country needs new housing," Karen said.

"No way!" Morgan laughed. He explained that departments always ask for more money than O.M.B. can give them. The president and the budget director trim each department's requests to a realistic level. Then, in January, the White House sends the budget for the coming fiscal year to Congress.

Morgan paused, seeing her puzzled look. "A fiscal year is a gov-

Executive Office Of The President

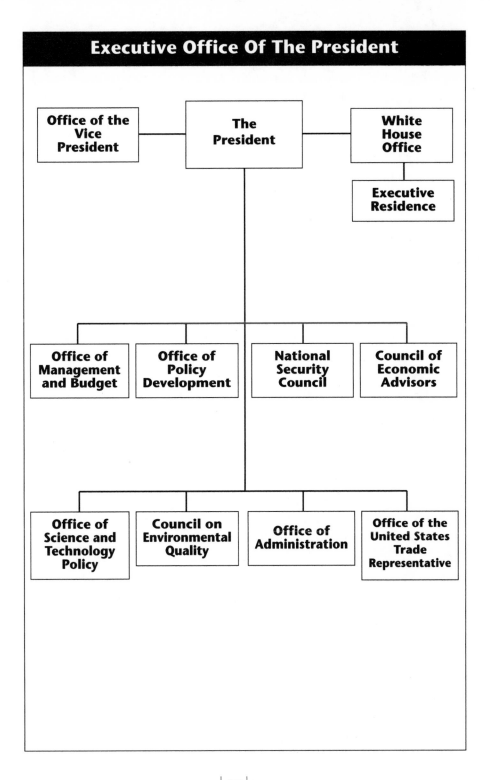

ernment invention," he told her. "It's a bookkeeping period that runs from October 1 to September 30 of the following year."

When she nodded her understanding, he went on. "When Congress gets the budget, it holds hearings. Everyone argues about who gets how much. Some of the O.M.B.'s hard work is ignored. But in the end, everyone agrees on a compromise budget. Then the House and Senate vote for the stack of appropriation bills that allow the government to pay its bills."

"And your job is over until next year," Karen observed.

Morgan assured her that O.M.B.'s job wasn't that simple. "Remember, the 'M' stands for Management," he said. "O.M.B. watches over the spending of more than a trillion dollars each year. We report to the president on how well each government agency is doing its job. When money is involved, we also help prepare the president's executive orders and veto messages."

Karen looked at her watch, gasped, and said a hurried goodby. She was supposed to meet Chet Billings in ten minutes.

An Efficient Operation

Karen made it to the chief of staff's office exactly at 3 o'clock. As she sat down and caught her breath, Billings described what he meant by "a crisis a day."

"The Chief Executive must stay in touch with everything that affects the United States," he said. "In the past week, we've had to cope with an earthquake in Alaska, an oil spill in Florida, and killer bees in Texas. On top of that, terrorists kidnapped one of our diplomats in the Middle East. The American people expect the president to deal promptly with all of these events. Even without a crisis or two, there's the daily crush of regular administrative detail."

Karen looked at all the notes she'd scribbled in such a short time. How could one person stay on top of everything?

Billings seemed to read her mind. He explained that the White House staff executes the president's wishes. If the Chief Executive wants to send emergency aid to Alaska, for example, all he has to do is say the word. Staff members contact the Emergency Management

Agency, which begins planning the relief shipments.

A picture of an efficient staff operation was taking shape in Karen's mind. Aides summarize vital national and world news and place their digests on the president's desk each morning. The chief of staff checks to make sure he's receiving the bad news as well as the good, because it's always tempting to shield the president from unpleasant realities. Even when flying in Air Force One, the president keeps in constant touch by radio. The Chief can call the White House, the Pentagon, the Kremlin in Moscow, or anyplace else in the world.

Each aide has a special area of responsibility. If a public statement is needed, the press secretary writes a news release or arranges a press conference. The counsel to the president provides legal advice.

"About 400 people serve on the White House staff," Billings concluded. "And from the looks of my calendar, every one of them is waiting to see me. Do you have everything you need?"

"I think so," Karen said. "Tomorrow I'm going to tackle the president's role as Chief Diplomat."

3

The President As Chief Diplomat

A taxi dropped Karen off at the huge, eight-story State Department building the next morning. She remembered that the area was known as Foggy Bottom, a reminder that Potomac River fogs had once settled there. The guard at the front desk looked at her White House pass and quickly confirmed her appointment. Three minutes later, Holly LaSalle appeared and accompanied Karen into an elevator and through a maze of corridors.

"I cleared my desk when Chet Billings told me you were coming," LaSalle said when they reached her office. "Do you want to be appointed as our ambassador to France?"

"No, I'd rather start with one of the smaller countries—Iceland, perhaps," Karen said with a laugh. "Actually, I'm here to learn more about the president's job as Chief Diplomat. It's for a visitors' handbook I'm writing for the White House."

The basic job of Chief Diplomat was easy for Ms. LaSalle to describe to Karen. The Constitution assigns the conduct of foreign affairs to the president, who appoints ambassadors to represent this country overseas. The president also receives foreign ambassadors who are assigned to Washington. He negotiates trade and military treaties. As a check on this power, the Senate must approve his appointments and treaties by a two-thirds vote. Beyond these requirements, the job of Chief Diplomat is further defined by law and custom.

Karen thought something was missing. "What about the State Department?" she asked. "Doesn't the Constitution mention it?"

"The Constitution doesn't mention any of the Cabinet departments," LaSalle replied. "It says only that the president may ask for the opinion of the 'principal officer in each of the executive departments.' Washington formed the first Cabinet in 1789. It was made up of three departments: State, Treasury and War. Thomas Jefferson served as the first secretary of state."

"Isn't it the secretary of state who directs U.S. foreign policy?" Karen wondered.

LaSalle shook her head. "I must emphasize that it's the president who directs foreign policy," she said. "The secretary of state and the State Department are only advisors when it comes to policy making. Right now the president is listening to our advice on the new trade treaty with Japan. Regardless of what he decides, it will be our job to carry out his policies."

Keeping The System In Balance

Karen thought about checks and balances. The Constitution gives each branch of government the power to "check" the other two. For two centuries the system has kept the legislative, judicial, and executive branches in balance. But the president is Chief Diplomat.

"Doesn't the Senate's right to approve or reject treaties upset that balance?"

LaSalle welcomed the question. "The Senate has turned down a number of treaties that various presidents wanted badly. President Carter, for example, couldn't win the two-thirds majority he needed to pass a treaty to limit the production of nuclear weapons."

"So, I'm right," Karen said. "Thirty-four senators can tie the president's hands when it comes to foreign policy."

LaSalle didn't agree. She described a strategy that emerged after the Senate rejected the treaty to annex Texas from Mexico in 1845. Its supporters turned the treaty into a "joint resolution" that needed only a simple majority of both houses. In that form, the resolution passed easily. President McKinley used the same method to annex Hawaii in 1898.

The Chief Diplomat also signs "executive agreements" that have the force of treaties. That practice began after World War II broke

Meeting world leaders to discuss the issues that concern nations is the president's
President Mikhail Gorbachev

...ob as chief diplomat for the United States. President George Bush and Soviet ...net in Malta in 1989.

Who Helps The President Plan A Trip?

Without the White House staff, the president could never get all his work done. Whether he's working quietly in the Oval Office or attending a summit conference, the staff must make sure that everything goes smoothly. Imagine that the president has scheduled a trip to California to sign a new trade treaty with the Japanese prime minister. Here are some of the White House offices that must swing into action to make the trip possible.

Office	Responsibility
Vice President	Briefs the president on what he learned during his recent trip to Japan.
Chief of Staff	Meets with representatives from Departments of State, Treasury, Commerce, and other agencies to coordinate their public statements supporting the treaty.
Trade Representative	Briefs president on strengths and weaknesses of treaty; attends talks to help negotiate final wording of the treaty.
Speechwriters	Draft the president's speeches, arrival and departure comments, and banquet toasts.

Office	Responsibility
Legal Counsel	Reviews the legal aspects of the treaty to insure that no laws will be violated.
Legislative Affairs Staff	Lines up congressional support for the treaty; invites friendly lawmakers to fly in for the treaty-signing ceremony.
Secret Service	Coordinates security arrangements with the California police. Ships bulletproof limo ahead, checks out routes, and runs security checks on people the president will meet.
Advance Office	Sends teams to California to arrange housing, transportation, and meeting and banquet facilities for the president's party.
Scheduling Office	Prepares detailed schedule covering every minute of the president's visit.
Press Office	Arranges briefings and interviews; coordinates media coverage of the signing ceremony.
Office of Public Liaison	Contacts pro-treaty trade and consumer groups to arrange lobbying efforts.

out in Europe, but while the United States was still neutral. President Roosevelt wanted to give 50 old Navy destroyers to the British, but he knew the Senate wouldn't approve. To avoid a losing fight, he traded the destroyers for the use of some British naval bases, and called it an executive agreement. Since then, many understandings between the president and foreign heads of state have been reached in this way.

"Can the Chief do that?" Karen looked a little shocked.

"The Supreme Court has ruled that executive agreements are legal," LaSalle said. "They're as binding as any treaty, even though Congress has no voice in approving or rejecting them."

Karen thought that this practice upset the balance in the President's favor.

"Could a weak President sign an executive agreement that would endanger the United States?"

LaSalle assured her that presidents simply do not have that much freedom.

"Even if they bypass the Senate, they must still answer to the American people. President Bush, for example, didn't ask for formal congressional approval before he sent troops into Panama in 1989. The successful landings were welcomed by the public and added greatly to his popularity. By contrast, President Carter's failed attempt to rescue American hostages from Iran in 1980 made him look weak. All presidents must take risks—but too many failures can cripple their ability to govern."

Planning A Summit Conference

Holly LaSalle called a halt to the interview and took Karen to the cafeteria for lunch. Afterward, an elevator carried them to the seventh floor. There, LaSalle pointed out the double glass doors that led to the Secretary of State's offices. As she did so, four men hurried past them and entered the office. They were speaking a language that Karen didn't recognize.

"Those Soviet diplomats are here to work out plans for next month's summit meeting," LaSalle explained. "The president and the secretary of state will be meeting face-to-face with the Soviet leaders. Top-level meetings give them a chance to cut through red tape and

Candidates for president used to be selected at the nominating conventions of the major political parties. With the development of the primary system, however, the candidates with the most delegates are usually known before the convention begins.

Air Force One is the

tackle long-standing problems. If all goes well, they'll reach compromises that might take years to negotiate at lower levels."

Karen knew that high-level conferences of this type were a fairly recent development. The United States took part in its first major summit conference after World War I. President Woodrow Wilson traveled to Paris in 1919 to work out a peace treaty with the French, British and Italian leaders. Wilson's goal was to create a peacekeeping

president's official jet.

organization called the League of Nations. The Senate, however, turned down the treaty. Joining the League of Nations would have forced the United States to take an active role in world affairs.

World War II forced the United States to give up its policy of staying isolated from Europe. During the war President Roosevelt revived the practice of summit meetings. He met several times with Winston Churchill of Great Britain and Josef Stalin of the Soviet Union. The meetings were useful for planning the strategy that won the war. But Roosevelt later was blamed for giving the Communists a free hand in controlling Eastern Europe after the war.

"Since World War II, we've held a number of summits," LaSalle said. "The results have been mixed. Some produced little more than bad feelings. Others have reduced the danger of nuclear war. President Nixon's trip to China in 1972, for instance, led to better relations with China's communist leaders."

LaSalle also told Karen that a summit conference was just the "tip of the iceberg."

"The less dramatic work of diplomacy goes on every day, scarcely noticed by the American people. The State Department in Washington serves as a nerve center for hundreds of embassies and consulates around the globe. In each overseas post, State Department officials are on duty to protect American interests."

What Is Diplomatic Recognition?

Karen followed Holly LaSalle through some of the building's six miles of corridors. By the time they returned to Holly's office, Karen's feet hurt. She envied the mail clerks, who rode small electric carts up and down the halls to make their deliveries.

A pattern was emerging. In his role as Chief Diplomat, the president made decisions about the nation's foreign policy. As Chief Executive, he supervised the conduct of those policies. How did this process work in practice? Karen asked LaSalle to imagine that a new country had just been created.

"I like that idea! How about calling it Jomoland?" LaSalle laughed. "As one of his first acts, King Nulla will ask the U.S. to extend diplomatic recognition. If he came to power legally, the president will probably agree. After the two countries exchange diplomats, they can negotiate treaties and trade freely with each other."

Karen understood that recognition doesn't always mean approval. For example, the United States recognizes Ethiopia, even though Americans hate the cruelties the Ethiopian government inflicts on its people. A speedy recognition of a new country can signify warm approval. In 1948, President Truman sent such a signal by recognizing Israel the same day it came into existence.

Recognition can also be withdrawn. What if King Nulla had been jailing U.S. citizens without cause? The president might respond by restricting diplomatic ties. First he would order our ambassador to come home, then he would put the armed forces on alert. The State Department would ask the king's diplomats to leave the U.S. At that point, the United Nations may step in to try to mend the dispute. In the language of diplomacy, a complete break in diplomatic relations is only a few steps short of war.

"I can see that keeping good diplomatic relations with other countries can be a full-time job," Karen said. She reread her notes, then looked up with a smile. "What does the State Department do in its spare time?" she asked.

LaSalle took the question seriously. "Whether the president needs information about Algeria or Zaire, there's a 'desk' here that has up-to-date answers," she said. "The desks are in constant contact with our embassies in capital cities all over the world. Our ambassadors and their staffs gather information, distribute aid, and work closely with the host governments. The United States also maintains consulates in many foreign cities. Consular officials have the job of promoting trade and helping American tourists who lose their passports or get into trouble with the local authorities."

When she left the State Department, Karen walked for a while beside the calm waters of the Tidal Basin. The quiet atmosphere under the fragrant cherry trees helped her unwind and think about the next day's interviews.

4

The President As Commander-In-Chief

Karen admired the snap and precision of the U.S. Marines who guarded the White House. Every move was precise, every uniform was perfect, every face was alert. She knew from her research that they were also highly skilled military personnel.

When she first saw Marine Captain Victor Smith, Karen felt as though she should salute. The captain met her at the door of his office looking very tall and military. He looked more human after he smiled and asked her to call him Vic.

Karen explained her mission. "I know the Constitution states that a civilian shall be Commander-in-Chief of the armed forces," she began. "Wouldn't a trained military officer do a better job?"

Vic told her that generals tend to be impatient with the slow workings of democratic government, and that freedom is better served by keeping the final military authority in the hands of a civilian Commander-in-Chief. To back up the president's authority, civilians also hold the top jobs in the Department of Defense.

The proof, Vic went on, is that the system works. A number of presidents began their careers as generals. But they exchanged their uniforms for civilian dress before they moved into the White House. The presidents from Kennedy to Bush weren't generals, but they all served in the armed forces during World War II.

Wherever the president goes, he is accompanied by the
Nuclear Launch Code Command Box, which allows the president
to launch a nuclear strike against another nation.
The commander-in-chief is never far from this reminder of war.

"I understand that," Karen said. "But you're making it sound as though presidents never get involved in military operations."

"The Commander-in-Chief is always involved," Vic said. He explained that President George Washington took personal command of American troops during the Whiskey Rebellion in 1794, when Pennsylvania farmers objected to new liquor taxes. Today's presidents are confined to setting policy and making decisions. Harry Truman liked to say, "The buck stops here." He meant that the president must make the really tough choices. It was Truman who gave the order to drop two atomic bombs on Japan at the end of World War II. In 1950, he also ordered U.S. forces to resist the Communist invasion of South Korea.

"More recently," Vic continued, "President Reagan sent troops into Grenada, and President Bush ordered landings in Panama to protect American interests. This country's enemies should never forget: the president has our armed forces behind him when he speaks."

Congress Holds The Purse Strings

Karen followed Captain Smith as he inspected his Marine sentries. Every uniform looked spotless to her, but Smith chewed out several men and woman for what he called "sloppy dress." Only the best can be Marines, he reminded them, and only the best Marines can serve at the White House.

After the inspection was over, they found seats in the White House Rose Garden. "Vic, if the president is Commander-in-Chief, where does Congress fit in?" Karen asked.

Vic took a moment to think about the question. "Our friends on Capitol Hill control the purse strings," he said at last. "The president and the Department of Defense must sell the military budget to Congress each year. During peacetime, it can be a hard sell. Many members would rather spend the money to educate kids, clean up the air, and replace aging bridges. But other members can see that the world is still a dangerous place. They know the military can't carry out its mission without expensive modern weapons. As a result of the competition for funds, the Department of Defense rarely gets everything it asks for."

"The President is asking for a big defense budget," Karen com-

One of the most famous election photos of the 20th century:
President Harry Truman shows a Chicago newspaper headline
that incorrectly announced that Truman had lost to his
Republican opponent, Thomas Dewey.

mented. She supported the lawmakers who wanted more money to clean up the environment.

Vic agreed that the yearly defense budget did seem high. But inflation can make the numbers seem larger than they really are. Every year Congress renews its debate on the proper percentage of the budget spent on defense.

Karen knew from her reading that Congress does more than control the budget. Its members also try to influence defense policy. The war in Vietnam was a good example. Angered by the seemingly endless war, Congress passed the War Powers Act. Under this new law the president was required to ask for approval of any lengthy military

When Is A War Not A War?

The Constitution spells out the nation's war-making powers quite clearly. The president is the Commander-in-Chief of the armed forces, but only Congress can declare war. A look at the history books shows that the United States has fought five "official wars." What about the other times that presidents have sent American forces into combat? Those have been either undeclared wars, police actions, or interventions. The scoreboard:

DECLARED WARS
Congress issued an official declaration of war for these five major American wars:
- War of 1812 (1812-1815)
- Mexican War (1846-1848)
- Spanish-American War (1898)
- World War I (1917-1918)
- World War II (1941-1945)

UNDECLARED WARS
America's undeclared wars have been fully as costly as those that have been declared. Political and diplomatic reasons, however, keep the government from issuing an official declaration of war. To declare war during the Civil War, for example, would have meant recognizing the Confederate States as an independent nation. The scoreboard:
- Civil War (1861-1865)
- Korean War (1950-1953)
- Vietnam War (1964-1973)

INTERVENTIONS AND POLICE ACTIONS (A SAMPLING)
Presidents have the authority to order military action by U.S. forces when they believe that failure to do so will endanger American citizens or American economic interests. As the following sampling shows, many of these interventions have taken place in Latin America. The scoreboard:

- Indian Wars (1800s)
- Philippine Islands (1899-1905)
- Panama (1903, 1964, 1989)
- Nicaragua (1912-1933)
- Mexico (1914, 1916-1917)
- Haiti (1915-1934)
- Dominican Republic (1916-1924, 1965)
- Lebanon (1958, 1983)
- Grenada (1983)

action. The action was needed, the law said, because only Congress has the power to declare war—and war hadn't been declared in Vietnam. This limit on fighting small, "brushfire" wars ended in 1983, when the Supreme Court ruled the War Powers Act unconstitutional.

"You're telling me that each branch of government should stick to what it does best," Karen summed up.

Vic nodded. "Congress can choose to fund the Stealth bomber or not. But once the decision is made, Congress is supposed to leave day-to-day management of our defenses to the Commander-in-Chief."

Keeping The Peace

Karen told the Marine captain about a magazine article she'd read where the author had described the anti-missile defenses built into the President's airliner. "Is the White House protected that carefully?" she wondered.

"Security at the White House is very tight," Vic said. "Washington police protect the gates, and anyone who enters uninvited sets off all kinds of alarms. The military guards the White House and the president's vacation retreat at Camp David. Secret Service agents guard his person wherever he goes. They also watch out for the First Family. Even so, presidents are hard to protect when they go out in public. It's hard to forget when assassins struck at Kennedy, Ford and Reagan."

"I see the problem," Karen said. "The people wouldn't like it if the president hid in the White House. So you worry about his safety while he makes himself accessible and stays in the public eye. And you hope that the defense policy decisions he makes will keep the country safe."

"Under the president's direction, the military constantly updates its defense plans," Vic agreed. "One leg, the military, relies on a strong, well-trained fighting force. Our missiles are ready to fly whenever the president gives the order. We'd never launch first, but our enemies know that if they attack us nothing can stop our counterattack from leveling their cities."

"No one would win a nuclear war," Karen said with a shudder.

"That's why our defense plan has two other legs," Vic assured her. "We build alliances with countries such as Great Britain and Germany in Europe, and Japan and South Korea in Asia. By combining our armed forces, we're all that much stronger. In addition, when friendly countries are threatened, we send them arms so they can protect themselves. We also send food, medicines, farm machinery and other aid to countries who need it. We don't always win friends with our aid, but people who have food and jobs are less likely to start a war."

Arms control and disarmament were two of Karen's favorite topics. She asked about the chances of reducing the risk of war by doing away with offensive missiles.

Vic cautioned that arms control agreements had to be carefully worded and enforced. He said he approved of the talks with the Soviets that were resulting in cutbacks on nuclear missiles. He also applauded the president's proposals to outlaw chemical and biological weapons.

"I hope the president and other world leaders do achieve arms control," he said. "If they do, we may be able to create a world free from the threat of war. Wouldn't that be a wonderful gift to leave to our children!"

The Department Of Defense

Karen flipped through her notes. "I've only investigated three of the president's seven jobs," she said, "and already I'm wondering how one person can do it all."

"The fact is, no one can," Vic said. "The president depends on his staff, the National Security Council, and the Department of Defense. Secretary of Defense Owens heads the D.O.D. from his headquarters in the Pentagon. He directs a million civilian employees and about two million military types like me."

The five-sided Pentagon lies on the far side of the Potomac River. Karen had read that it was the world's largest office building. One of the jokes among Pentagon employees was that new employees who lost their way in its 17.5 miles of corridors were never seen again.

The president appoints senior generals and admirals to the Pentagon's Joint Chiefs of Staff. The Joint Chiefs have the task of keeping the armed forces in a high state of readiness. Usually they work well together, but interservice rivalries can be a problem. If the Navy and the Air Force can't agree on a new radar system, for example, the president may be called on to settle the dispute.

"Military decisions are never made in a vacuum," Vic said. "Let's say Panama's army tries to take over that country's government. The Pentagon gives advice on how to defend the Panama Canal. The Central Intelligence Agency adds information gathered from its network of satellites and spies. The State Department chips in with its best judgment of how other nations will react to our sending troops into Panama. The civilian and military members of the National Security Council then translate it all into military options for the President to consider."

"I have time for one last question," Karen said. "Tell me about the 'military-industrial complex.'"

"That's a way of saying that the Pentagon and the nation's defense contractors are too friendly," Vic told her. He explained that the problem starts when officers retire and go to work for defense companies. They use their contacts in the Pentagon to win high-profit contracts for their new bosses. As a result, the public gets a big tax bill and the military gets stuck with overpriced weapons—some of which don't work.

Geraldine Ferraro became the first woman ever to win a nomination to run for vice president. She shared the ticket in 1984 with former vice president Walter Mondale. Their bid for the highest offices in the land was defeated by the reelection of Ronald Reagan and George Bush.

"That's terrible!" Karen exclaimed. She'd read stories of hundred-dollar screws and missiles that wouldn't fly straight.

"It's getting better," Smith said. "The government is watching contractors more carefully. A few companies have been forced to pay huge fines. In the end, though, it's up to the Commander-in-Chief. If he's upset, he can switch to his role as Chief Legislator. Then he can lobby Congress for tougher laws."

5

The President As Chief Legislator

T he title on Marion Watney's door read Special Assistant to the President for Legislative Affairs. She greeted Karen warmly and motioned her to sit down.

"Your job must seem strange to many people," Karen said. "Most people don't think of the president as having much to do with legislation. They only see him signing bills after they're passed by Congress."

"Very few bills go through Congress without some input from the president," Watney explained. "My staff and I keep watch on every major bill that's introduced. We support the ones we think will be good for the country. And we fight the ones we think will cause trouble if Congress passes them."

Karen looked a little surprised. "Doesn't a Chief Legislator do more than react to what others do?"

"Do you remember the long list of promises the president made during his election campaign?" Mrs. Watney asked. "Now that he's in office, the voters expect him to keep his word. To do that, we're trying to push bills through Congress that will turn his promises into reality."

"A president's ability to inspire new legislation is one measure of his success," Watney explained. "Strong presidents with good ideas usually find support for their programs in Congress. Sometimes bills

*Protest is an American tradition, and citizens often gather
in the nation's capital to let the president and their congressmen
known where they should stand on specific issues.
Rallys and marches such as this one are commonplace in Washington, D.C.*

are drafted by the White House and given to friendly lawmakers to introduce. But more often, members of the president's party draft the bills with his approval.

"The President's legislative powers don't stop there," she continued. "Yesterday the White House issued two executive orders. One set up new flight paths for jetliners, and the other spelled out training procedures for Peace Corps volunteers."

"Are executive orders constitutional?" Karen was remembering her earlier discussion of executive agreements with Holly LaSalle.

"They're not mentioned in the Constitution," Watney said. "But they're legal because the president uses them to carry out his constitutional powers. He also issues them to interpret and enforce the laws passed by Congress. There are over 10,000 executive orders on the books right now. The Supreme Court would have thrown them out long ago if they weren't legal."

With that, she stood up and reached for her coat. "Come on," she said. "I have work to do on Capitol Hill."

Lining Up Votes On Capitol Hill

For the next two hours Karen tagged along as Marion Watney visited one lawmaker after another. In each office, the White House aide asked for a "yes" vote on the truck safety bill that was coming up for debate.

As they talked to various lawmakers, Karen saw the system of checks and balances in operation. The president had opened the campaign for this bill by inserting a promise to improve truck safety in his State of the Union message. Later, he set money aside in the budget to pay for the new brake inspection program. Only Congress has the power to make the laws, but the members can't ignore a popular president's wishes. Watney warned doubtful members that the public would bury them in angry letters if they voted against the president.

"The president isn't leaving anything undone," Mrs. Watney said. "Secretary of Transportation Bell will be here this afternoon to add more weight to our lobbying. If that's not enough, the president will start working the phone."

Karen knew the president's reputation. He often called legislators and turned on the full force of his personality. It took a stubborn lawmaker to resist the president when he said, "I'm counting on you to help pass this bill."

"What if the phone calls don't work?" Karen asked.

"The president has two more weapons—patronage and the pork barrel," Watney said. "Patronage is the power to appoint people to federal jobs that aren't covered by civil service. Lawmakers love patronage because they can pay off favors and put friends in good jobs. The

President Ronald Reagan made a dramatic point about the cumbersome federal budget process during his 1988 State of the Union address. The legislative and executive branches must compromise annually to produce a budget that meets the costs of government.

"pork barrel" is filled with projects that are a way of rewarding party loyalty by paying for federal projects in a lawmaker's home state. No one likes to admit that it exists, but it's a fact of political life. Voters reelect representatives who look out for their interests."

Karen saw that Watney "spent" these favors carefully. When she could, she talked lawmakers into voting for the bill by arguing its good points. If they still resisted, she told them that the president was depending on them.

One senator shook his head. The truckers in his state, he said, were dead set against the bill. But he changed his mind when Watney reminded him that his state needed a new flood-control dam. The promise of White House support for the dam won his vote.

When they were alone, Karen asked, "What will the president say when you tell him you made that deal with Senator Hill?"

The legislative aide shrugged. "What the senator doesn't know won't hurt him," she said. "The president told me yesterday that he's already approved the building of that dam."

The Press Conference

At one o'clock Karen and Marion Watney hurried back to the White House to watch a presidential press conference. Karen was amazed by the number of reporters who crowded into the room.

"What's happening?" she whispered.

"The president told his press secretary to call this conference," Watney answered. "He's probably going to appeal to the voters to support the truck safety bill."

Many presidents have used the media to reach out to the American people. One of the best at the game was President Harry Truman. In 1948, no one gave him much hope of winning reelection. Truman took his case to the people, charging that the country was badly served by a "do-nothing" Congress. The public liked his fiery style and swept him back into the White House.

A man in a rumpled suit was adjusting the microphones at the speaker's podium. Karen recognized him as the press secretary. Tom Plowright had once been a network television reporter. Now, with the

Which Presidents Had The Highest Veto Batting Average?

When presidents take on the role of Chief Legislator, the veto becomes one of their most powerful weapons. Any attempt to override the veto leads to a tough battle in Congress—and the president usually wins. This table charts the "batting averages" of the presidents who have completed their terms in the White House during this century.

President	Vetoes	Overrides	Percentage Vetoes Sustained
Theodore Roosevelt	82	1	.988
William H. Taft	39	1	.974
Woodrow Wilson	44	6	.864
Warren G. Harding	6	0	1.000
Calvin Coolidge	50	4	.920
Herbert Hoover	37	3	.919
Franklin D. Roosevelt	635	9	.986
Harry S Truman	250	12	.952
Dwight D. Eisenhower	181	2	.989
John F. Kennedy	21	0	1.000
Lyndon B. Johnson	30	0	1.000
Richard M. Nixon	42	5	.881
Gerald R. Ford	66	12	.818
Jimmy Carter	29	2	.931
Ronald W. Reagan	78	9	.897

help of his staff, he managed the president's contacts with the media. He issued news releases, scheduled press conferences, and set up "photo opportunities."

Photo "ops" are picture-taking sessions that keep the president in the public eye. In a typical photo op, the president appears in the Rose Garden and awards a medal to a heroic police officer. Everyone smiles, cameras record the scene, and it's over before reporters can ask any in-depth questions.

Karen could see how important the media was to the Chief Legislator. This campaign to pass the truck safety bill was a good example. The press conference was carrying the president's voice into living rooms all over America. Later the press office would release a poll paid for by the president's party. Watney guessed that the poll would show people favoring the bill by a 3-to-2 margin. In addition, the staff was asking consumer groups to flood Congress with letters.

Everyone stood as the president walked briskly into the room. Karen whispered, "What if the reporters ask a question the president isn't prepared for?"

"The press secretary rehearses the president," Watney said. He plays the role of a reporter, asking all the questions the staff thinks will be fired at the president. Even if they guess wrong, the president is quick on his feet. He knows how to give soft answers that sound good but don't say much."

The Veto Is A Powerful Weapon

The press conference was going smoothly. The president made a strong case for the truck safety bill and answered a few questions. Then, just as the press secretary signaled that time was up, a reporter caught the president's eye.

"Mr. President," the woman said, "will you sign the hospital construction bill that Congress passed last week?"

The smile vanished from the president's face. "You know and I know that the hospital bill is a budget-buster," he snapped. "We can't afford it. I told Congress that I would veto the bill if it passed, and veto it I shall!"

With that, the president turned and left. As the reporters rushed to file their stories, Karen turned to Watney.

"This president isn't afraid to use the veto," she said. "Is it because the other party's in control of Congress?"

Watney said no. She explained that the all-time veto champs were Franklin Roosevelt and Harry Truman. They used the veto freely even though their party controlled Congress for most of the years they were in office. More often, presidents only have to threaten to veto a certain bill. Hearing that threat, Congress allows the bill to die quietly. "I know it takes a two-thirds vote of both houses to override a veto," Karen said. "How often does Congress override?"

"Vetoes are upheld almost nine times out of ten," Watney replied. "Some presidents have done much better. Eisenhower vetoed 181 bills with only two overrides. Kennedy and Johnson were never overridden."

Karen thought about the two types of vetoes. Normally, presidents veto a bill and send Congress a message that explains why they did so. Then it's up to Congress to try to override the veto. If the members do so, the bill becomes law. If they can't override, the bill dies. At the end of a session, presidents can use the "pocket veto." This means that if they haven't signed a bill at the end of ten days (not counting Sundays), the bill dies.

"The veto is really a powerful weapon," Karen observed.

"Yes, but it's more like a club than a scalpel," Watney said. "Presidents must either approve or reject the entire bill. They can't veto parts of a bill, as some governors can. But it will take a constitutional amendment to give them the 'item veto.' As it is now, our Chief Legislator often accepts a problem bill rather than have no bill at all."

6

The President As Chief Jurist

Karen caught up with Frederick Tuttle as he was striding down the hallway with an armload of files. He turned when she called to him, his walrus mustache bristling.

"Miss Rossi?" he boomed. "Wait in my office. Haven't got all day. Chet Billings knows how busy I am."

Tuttle bounded off as Karen watched him go. Billings had forgotten to warn her that the director of presidential appointments was a human dynamo.

Karen had a question ready when Tuttle returned. She was about to ask him to describe the president's role in appointing federal judges when the phone rang.

Tuttle grabbed the phone and Karen sat back in the big leather chair. As she waited she reviewed the reading she'd been doing. The job of Chief Jurist was part of the system of checks and balances. The president "checks" the judicial branch by exercising several constitutional powers. All federal judges, from the Chief Justice of the Supreme Court on down, owe their appointments to the president. The president also appoints the head of the F.B.I. and other top federal law enforcement officials. These are the officials the president depends on to carry out court orders and enforce court decisions. Finally, the president is given the power to grant pardons.

Modern presidential politics changed forever with the first broadcast of a debate on national television. John F. Kennedy and Richard Nixon faced each other in this Chicago studio as millions of voters watched in their living rooms.

Karen saw that Tuttle had put down the phone and was drumming his fingers on the desk. "Why is the power to nominate federal judges so important?" she asked quickly.

"Once appointed, federal judges keep their jobs for life," Tuttle told her. "They can only be removed by death, retirement, or impeachment. That's why presidents try to choose judges whose ideas agree with theirs. They know that the judges they appoint will be deciding cases long after they leave the White House."

"How do presidents make their choices?" Karen inquired.

Tuttle tapped his pile of files. "That's my job," he said. "I collect files on candidates suggested by the Justice Department, the American Bar Association, and members of Congress. Of course, the president isn't bound by their recommendations. He may use the appointment to pay off a political debt or to reward a faithful ally. Once he makes his decision, the nomination goes to the Senate."

Winning Confirmation In The Senate

Karen remembered the president's fight with the Senate over his last Supreme Court appointment. After a long battle, the President had been forced to withdraw the nomination of Judge Yates. She asked Tuttle to explain.

Tuttle paced up and down as he talked. "Historically, the Senate has rejected one out of every five Supreme Court nominees," he said. "Don't forget, the nominees aren't just anybody. They're leading attorneys, legal scholars, and well-known judges from state and federal courts. The Senate is supposed to examine their personal and legal qualifications. More and more, however, senators study the nominees' political philosophy as well. Judge Yates had an excellent legal mind, but many of his prior decisions had gone against minority groups. His record ran counter to the beliefs of many senators and cost him the nomination."

"Does the president lobby for his nominees the way he lobbies for a bill?" Karen inquired.

Tuttle shook his head. He explained that the Senate guards its independence fiercely. Senators may throw out a nomination if the president pushes too hard, but a determined president has his own weapons. The White House can issue press releases that praise the nominee's strong points. The staff can schedule friendly witnesses to testify during the confirmation hearings. In the end, the vote often follows political lines. A nominee who is too liberal or too conservative is likely to be rejected.

"Let's suppose that the president does win the battle in the Senate," Karen said. "How does he know that the new judge will fulfill his expectations?"

"Coattails"—or in this case, horsetails—are often mentioned as a factor in a successful presidential campaign. This 1908 political cartoon implies that William Howard Taft was elected president thanks to his close ties to former president Theodore Roosevelt.

Who's Been Sitting At The President's Desk?

George Bush became the forty-first president of the United States when he moved into the White House in 1989. The chart below lists all of the men who have held the nation's highest office. Some rank

	Name	Age	Occupation
1.	George Washington	57	Planter/Soldier
2.	John Adams	61	Lawyer
3.	Thomas Jefferson	58	Planter/Lawyer
4.	James Madison	57	Planter
5.	James Monroe	58	Planter/Lawyer
6.	John Quincy Adams	57	Diplomat
7.	Andrew Jackson	61	Planter/Soldier
8.	Martin Van Buren	54	Lawyer
9.	William Harrison	68	Soldier
10.	John Tyler	51	Lawyer
11.	James K. Polk	49	Lawyer
12.	Zachary Taylor	64	Planter/Soldier
13.	Millard Fillmore	50	Teacher/Lawyer
14.	Franklin Pierce	48	Lawyer
15.	James Buchanan	65	Lawyer
16.	Abraham Lincoln	52	Lawyer
17.	Andrew Johnson	56	Tailor
18.	Ulysses S. Grant	46	Soldier
19.	Rutherford B. Hayes	54	Lawyer
20.	James A. Garfield	49	Teacher
21.	Chester A. Arthur	50	Teacher/Lawyer
22.	Grover Cleveland	47	Lawyer
23.	Benjamin Harrison	55	Lawyer
24.	Grover Cleveland	55	Lawyer
25.	William McKinley	54	Lawyer
26.	Theodore Roosevelt	42	Rancher/Soldier
27.	William H. Taft	51	Lawyer
28.	Woodrow Wilson	56	Professor
29.	Warren Harding	55	Newspaper Publisher
30.	Calvin Coolidge	51	Lawyer
31.	Herbert Hoover	54	Engineer
32.	Franklin Roosevelt	50	Lawyer
33.	Harry S Truman	60	Farmer/Merchant
34.	Dwight Eisenhower	62	Soldier
35.	John F. Kennedy	43	Politician
36.	Lyndon Johnson	55	Teacher/Politician
37.	Richard Nixon	56	Lawyer
38.	Gerald R. Ford	61	Lawyer
39.	Jimmy Carter	52	Farmer/Businessman
40.	Ronald Reagan	69	Actor/Politician
41.	George Bush	64	Oilman/Politician

• Age at the time they were inaugurated.

among the greatest Americans who have ever lived. Others are
scarcely remembered.

Party	Birthplace	Years Served
Federalist	Virginia	1789-1797
Federalist	Massachusetts	1797-1801
Democratic-Republican	Virginia	1801-1809
Democratic-Republican	Virginia	1809-1817
Democratic-Republican	Virginia	1817-1825
Democratic-Republican	Massachusetts	1825-1829
Democrat	South Carolina	1829-1837
Democrat	New York	1837-1841
Whig	Ohio	1841
Whig	Virginia	1841-1845
Democrat	North Carolina	1845-1849
Whig	Virginia	1849-1850
Whig	New York	1850-1853
Democrat	New Hampshire	1853-1857
Democrat	Pennsylvania	1857-1861
Republican	Illinois	1861-1865
National Union	North Carolina	1865-1869
Republican	Illinois	1869-1877
Republican	Ohio	1877-1881
Republican	Ohio	1881
Republican	Vermont	1881-1885
Democrat	New Jersey	1885-1889
Republican	Ohio	1889-1893
Democrat	New Jersey	1893-1897
Republican	Ohio	1897-1901
Republican	New York	1901-1909
Republican	Ohio	1909-1913
Democrat	Virginia	1913-1921
Republican	Ohio	1921-1923
Republican	Vermont	1923-1929
Republican	Iowa	1929-1933
Democrat	New York	1933-1945
Democrat	Missouri	1945-1953
Republican	Texas	1953-1961
Democrat	Massachusetts	1961-1963
Democrat	Texas	1963-1969
Republican	California	1969-1974
Republican	Michigan	1974-1977
Democrat	Georgia	1977-1981
Republican	Illinois	1981-1989
Republican	Massachusetts	1989-

Tuttle's eyes narrowed. "Judges seldom vote with the president on every case!" he boomed. "Their lifetime appointments make them immune to popular opinion and political influence. About one Supreme Court justice in four does an almost complete turnaround. 'Conservatives' become 'liberals,' and vice versa. Putting on a judge's robes can change a person."

As Karen's pencil raced across the page, Tuttle listed the reasons judges change.

"Sometimes it's their sense of duty to the Constitution. Maybe they decide to work for higher standards of justice. Contact with the brilliant men and women who share the bench with them can also influence their rulings. Remember," he concluded, "no one can force federal judges to violate their consciences."

The Power To Pardon

Karen looked through her notes to see if she had missed anything. "Once a judge is appointed, it looks as though the president's power to check the judicial branch ends," she said. "He can't veto a Supreme Court decision."

"That's right," Tuttle agreed. "But you're forgetting the power to pardon. The president can use it to cancel decisions made in the federal courts. Someone convicted in a state court must appeal to the governor of the state for a pardon."

Karen thought about the technical terms connected with pardons. A pardon, she knew, is legal forgiveness for a crime. A full pardon restores all civil rights, including the right to vote and hold office. Most presidential pardons are given after someone has been tried and convicted. But the president can grant a pardon even before a case comes to trial. In 1974, President Ford pardoned former President Nixon for "all offenses against the United States"—even though Nixon hadn't been charged with any of the Watergate crimes. Those who accept pardons under these conditions are, in effect, admitting their guilt.

Tuttle's fingers were drumming again. Karen asked quickly, "I understand the idea of a pardon. But what are reprieves, commuted sentences, and amnesty?"

The older man ticked off the points one by one. A reprieve delays the carrying out of a sentence, he explained. The delay can postpone anything from a death sentence to a heavy fine. The reprieve is only temporary, but it gives the courts time to restudy the case. To commute a sentence or a fine is to reduce its severity. For example, he said, the president commuted a sentence last week that reduced a life sentence to a ten-year term. The prisoner's lawyers convinced him that the original punishment was unfair.

"That leaves amnesty," Karen prodded.

"Think of amnesty as a general pardon given to an entire group of people. In 1977, President Jimmy Carter issued an amnesty for over 10,000 Vietnam-era draft evaders."

"I can see that granting pardons might not make everyone happy," Karen said.

"Carter upset a lot of people with that amnesty," he said. "But, as Harry Truman liked to say, 'If you can't take the heat, get out of the kitchen.' A president has to do what he thinks is right, not what's popular."

Defying The Courts

Karen could see that Tuttle was anxious to get back to his work. She thanked him and was almost out the door when she remembered a final point.

"Earlier, you said that the president also carries out court decisions," she said. "What if he disagrees with the decision? Is he bound to obey the courts?"

Tuttle sighed and thumbed through a worn copy of the Constitution. He pointed to the Oath of Office. "Each President swears to 'faithfully execute the office of President of the United States.' That's a fine pledge but it hasn't always been kept. In 1832, for example, the Supreme Court ruled that the federal treaties with the Cherokees in Georgia must be upheld. President Andrew Jackson believed that upholding the treaties would violate states' rights. Jackson had roared, 'John Marshall [the Chief Justice] has made his decision. Now let him

Voters cast their ballots for the candidate they feel will make the best president. Candidates start campaiging more than a year before the election, so voters have a long time to decide which person should hold the highest office in the United States.

enforce it.' Jackson won that contest of wills. Within a few years the Cherokees were forced to give up their land and move to Oklahoma."

"That was a long time ago," Karen said. "Modern presidents don't defy the courts, do they? I know that President Nixon didn't. When the Supreme Court ruled against him, he handed over the Watergate tapes to Congress. He must have done so knowing that evidence on the tapes could lead to his impeachment."

"There are different ways of defying the Supreme Court," Tuttle told her. "One way is to delay the execution of a court order. In the 1954 case of *Brown v. Board of Education*, for example, the Supreme

Court ordered an end to segregated public schools. President Eisenhower was supposed to enforce the ruling, but critics say he acted too slowly. As a result, some schools remained segregated by race for many years."

Karen shook hands with Tuttle and walked slowly back to her office. As she looked through her notes, she thought that "Chief Jurist" might not be the best title. The job could also be called Chief Administrator of Justice.

A thought struck her and she pulled out her government manual. There it was, the Department of Justice. The cabinet-level department was headed by the Attorney General. It included the F.B.I., the Drug Enforcement Administration, the Immigration and Naturalization Service, and the Bureau of Prisons.

It's fortunate the Chief Jurist has help, she told herself. Otherwise, he wouldn't have time to serve as Chief Politician.

7

The President As Chief Politician

Karen studied her list of White House staffers for a long time. Who could she interview about the job of Chief Politician? Finally she gave up and called Chet Billings.

The chief of staff listened to her problem and thought for a moment. Then he said, "Go over to the party's national headquarters. I'll call Rose Simpson and let her know you're coming."

A taxi took Karen to the headquarters on First Street. Rose Simpson was waiting for her in her office.

"It struck me as I was coming over here," Karen said. "Of all the president's jobs, this is the only one that I can't trace back to some legal basis in the Constitution."

Simpson nodded her agreement. She explained that political parties didn't exist when the Constitution was written. George Washington looked at England's parties and hoped the same idea wouldn't take root in the United States. He believed they did little more than divide a country into warring camps. Despite his warnings, however, the first American parties appeared during the struggle to ratify the Constitution. By 1800, the two-party system was well established. Each party supported its own candidates for Congress and for the presidency.

"What is the president's role within the party?" Karen asked.

Simpson pointed to the picture of the president that hung from her wall. "The president is the head of our party," she said. "But that doesn't mean that he dictates party policies. Our members are free to disagree with the president and with this headquarters. Besides, successful presidents see themselves as leaders of all Americans, not just their party."

Karen looked puzzled. "In that case, is it really fair to say that the president is our Chief Politician?"

Simpson closed her eyes and thought for a moment. "Almost everything the president does is political in one way or another," she said at last. "If he can't charm you into agreeing with his policies, he'll twist your arm until you do. In addition, the president picks the party's national officials. That keeps the party faithful to him and insures that the work will get done. We handle fundraising and publicity, put on voter registration drives, and organize the national party convention. We also support the party's candidates in local and state elections."

Wooing Reluctant Voters

Karen felt confused. Hesitantly, she asked, "How does the president keep from mixing politics into his other duties?"

"The dividing line between political and nonpolitical duties often gets blurred," Simpson said. "If the president flies to Maine to inspect a nuclear power plant, that's clearly an official duty. While he's there, however, he may invite the party's candidate for governor to share the speaker's platform with him. All at once, a business trip becomes a political event as well. It's the president's 'Superman' act. Without stepping into a phone booth, he changes from Chief Executive to Chief Politician."

Karen thought of a cartoon showing politicians riding into office on the president's coattails. Could a president's support still carry a candidate to victory? Simpson told her that presidential coattails had lost much of their magic. She pointed out that since 1968, Republicans had held the White House for 20 out of 24 years. Despite that, the Democrats never lost control of the House of Representatives during those years. In addition, the president's party almost always loses seats in the "off year" elections between presidential elections.

Politics is a strange business, Karen told herself. "If voters approve

of a president, why don't they vote for his party's congressional candidates?" she asked.

"My job would be a lot easier if I knew the answer to that question," Simpson laughed. "All I know is what our surveys tell us. For one thing, Americans are independent thinkers. Many people vote for the candidate they think is the best choice, regardless of party labels. Also, there's the problem of district boundaries. The majority party in the state legislatures tends to create districts where their party has a

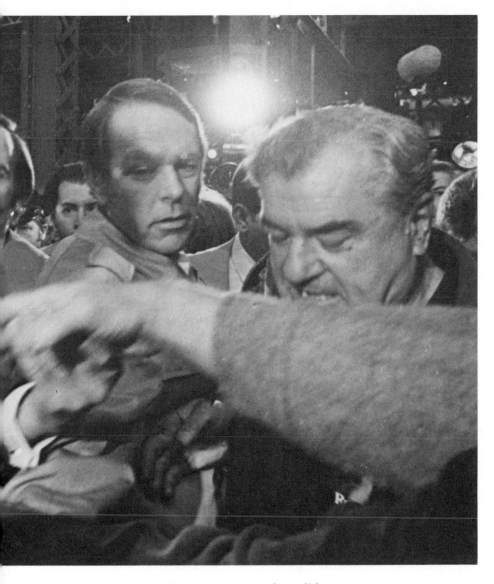

A president is a perpetual candidate.

safe edge in numbers. The minority party almost never wins an election in one of those gerrymandered districts."

"I've heard that some voters can't tell the difference between the two parties," Karen said.

Simpson frowned. "I can give you a dozen differences between my party and the opposition," she said. Then she sighed. "But you're right. The average voter couldn't care less about my list of differences. Both parties say they're for peace and prosperity. Both say they're against crime and high taxes. It's no wonder most voters ignore a president's endorsement. People are more interested in how the candidate will solve the local trash disposal problem."

Choosing A Vice President

Mrs. Simpson paused to answer the telephone. Karen tried not to listen, but she couldn't help hearing the vice president's name. How had the president picked his running mate?

When Simpson put down the phone she saw the question in Karen's eyes. "You're wondering about the vice president, aren't you?" she said. "Many people think our method of choosing the president's possible successor is incredibly careless."

"Well, you'd think that vice presidents would be chosen for their ability, not for political reasons," Karen said.

Simpson shook her head. "Presidential candidates never admit that politics influence their choice of a running mate," she said. "Besides, the theory is that delegates to the party's national convention select the candidates. In actual practice, they usually support the presidential candidate's choice."

Political experts refer to the art of choosing the V.P. candidate as "ticket-balancing." Parties don't want to lose votes because some segment of the population feels left out. If the presidential candidate comes from the Sunbelt, an easterner will probably be picked for the second slot. Farm state nominees are balanced with candidates from industrial states. In 1984, Walter Mondale made history by picking Congresswoman Geraldine Ferraro as his running mate. Ferraro was the first woman nominated for vice president by a major party.

Karen looked at her notes. "Do presidential candidates ever pick their rivals to run with them?"

"It happens," Simpson said. "By picking a strong rival, the candidate hopes to unite the party behind him. That's why John Kennedy chose Lyndon Johnson in 1960. He needed Johnson's southern supporters. 'Political marriages' do sometimes succeed, but they're not common. In the heat of a primary campaign, the candidates often make harsh statements about each other. How can you team up with

In the 1988 presidential race Senator Dan Quayle of Indiana was a surprise choice as George Bush's running mate. The Bush-Quayle ticket defeated Michael Dukakis, the governor of Massachusetts, and Quayle was inaugurated as the new vice president in 1989.

Who Elects The President?

Every four years, Americans go to the polls to elect their presidents. Most voters believe that it's their ballots that elect the winners, but that's not quite true. According to the Constitution, the people are actually voting for a slate of electors. Six weeks after the general election, the electors gather as an Electoral College to cast their ballots for president. Only when Congress meets in joint session to open these ballots is the president officially selected.

Question	Answer
Why do we have the Electoral College?	The framers of the Constitution didn't trust the people to make intelligent choices when they voted. The framers also believed that electors would be needed to select a winner from the large field of candidates they thought would run for president. In their view, no one person was likely to win a majority of the popular vote.
Which state has the most electoral votes (out of the 538 that candidates compete for)?	Each state is entitled to as many electoral votes as it has senators and representatives. Every state has two senators, but the number of representatives is based on population. Thus, in 1988, California had 47 electoral votes, Texas had 29, and Alaska had 3. The District of Columbia is given 3 electoral votes, even though it is not a state.

Question	Answer
Can a president be elected without winning the popular vote?	Normally, the electoral vote reflects the popular vote. But John Quincy Adams, Rutherford B. Hayes, and Benjamin Harrison were elected after receiving fewer popular votes than their opponents. Several other elections have come within a handful of votes of ending in the same way.
What happens if no candidate wins a majority of the electoral vote?	If no one receives a majority of the electoral vote, the election must be decided in the House of Representatives. There, each state has one vote. Only two elections have been thrown into the House—the elections of 1800 and 1824. When this occurs, the party that controls the House has the power to pick its own candidate to be president.
Will the Electoral College system be changed?	The Electoral College system has been criticized as being undemocratic, but it has been changed only once. In 1804, the Twelfth Amendment clarified the way in which the vice president is elected. Over 500 amendments aimed at revising the system have been introduced in Congress, but none has been submitted to the states for ratification.

someone who's been saying you're 'soft on crime, soft on taxes, and soft in the head'?"

Karen smiled at the image. "Do vice presidential candidates see the job as a stepping stone to the presidency?" she asked.

"Their best bet is to inherit the office after a president dies," Simpson said. "They haven't done as well running on their own. Martin Van Buren made it in 1836. After that, no incumbent vice president won the White House until George Bush was elected in 1988. Richard Nixon earns a footnote, however. He was vice president when he lost in 1960, but he came back to win in 1968."

The Media And The Chief Politician

After she left Simpson's office, Karen wandered around the headquarters building. After poking her head into a number of offices, she found her way to the press office.

A red-haired young man was staring at a computer screen. He tapped out a few words, paused, and then hit the delete key. "I'll never get it right," he muttered. The nameplate on his desk said he was Jason Kaufman.

"What's the problem?" Karen asked. She showed Jason her White House pass and explained her mission.

Jason gave her a weary smile. "I'm preparing a mailer to send to our party's big contributors. It isn't easy to explain to auto dealers why the president signed the new trade agreement with Japan. They've already heard reports from the media that the treaty is a sellout of American business interests."

It looked to Karen as though the media both loved and hated the president. During interviews, television and newspaper reporters laughed at his jokes and asked their questions in respectful tones. But those same reporters often turned critical when they wrote their stories. One network commentator had angrily described the president as a captive of Japanese business interests.

"I see the problem," Karen said. "But I've also seen the president use the media for his own purposes. Just this week, he called a press conference to promote the truck safety bill."

"Yeah, each side needs the other," Jason said. "Our Chief Politician needs publicity and the media need stories. Of course, some presidents handle the press better than others. President Reagan was wonderful when he spoke from a prepared text. But he sometimes got flustered with questions he hadn't rehearsed ahead of time. This president talks well without notes, so he's usually available to reporters."

"The press secretary told the interns that the president is something of a captive to the media," Karen said.

Jason shrugged. "That's true during election campaigns," he said. "You can't win votes without media coverage. But once you're in office, you call the shots. Everything you do is news. That's why reporters are always on duty in the White House Press Room. It's the Chief Politician who holds the media captive, believe me."

As Karen turned to leave, Jason called her back. He invited her to a concert that night in the East Room of the White House. "If you say yes," he urged, "I'll introduce you to the president!"

8

The President As Chief of State

Jason led Karen into the East Room a half hour before the concert was to start. Although a popular country-western group was slated to perform, everyone wore evening dress. Karen looked around and breathed a sigh of relief. Thanks to her training lectures, she was dressed properly.

"Come over here and meet Deborah Wingate," Jason said. "She can be your expert on the president's job as Chief of State."

"What's her position?" Karen whispered.

"Deborah works in the Office of the Chief of Protocol," Jason told her. "That's the office that advises the president and the White House staff on the fine points of diplomatic behavior. After all, as Chief of State the president represents the power and dignity of the nation. We wouldn't want him to offend the Queen of England by calling her by her first name."

Jason introduced Karen to Deborah and excused himself to talk to Chet Billings. Even though it was a social evening, Karen decided to press on with her investigation.

"Compared to Chief of State, the president's other jobs seem much more important," she said. "Surely the president can't afford to devote much time to ceremonial duties."

Deborah was quick to correct Karen's mistaken impression. "As Chief of State the president plays host to important foreign leaders,"

All presidents are politicians, and that means they all have to "press the flesh" once in awhile. Here, President and Mrs. Bush meet some of their neighbors in Kennebunkport, Maine.

A political milestone was reached in 1988 when the Rev. Jesse Jackson became the first African-American to win a significant portion of the delegates at the Democratic Party Convention.

she said. "A visit from a prime minister calls for state dinners, complete with a reception line and hundreds of guests. And that's not all. The President signs the commissions of all military officers, down to second lieutenants. In a typical day he may be called on to greet a champion soccer team, a charity's poster child, and a space shuttle crew."

"Can't the vice president take over some of the duties?" Karen managed to ask.

"The president does use the vice president as a stand-in for ceremonial duties," Deborah said. "Last month, for example, the vice president represented the United States at a state funeral in Asia. But there are many traditions that the president wouldn't dare break. For example, he attends the Easter Egg Roll on the White House lawn and throws out the first ball to open the baseball season. Who else could lay the wreath on the Tomb of the Unknown Soldier on Veterans Day? The entire nation sees itself reflected in the person of the president on these ceremonial occasions."

A Job Only The President Can Do

Jason caught Karen's hand and pulled her away. She managed to smile her thanks at Deborah as he said, "Let's find our seats. The president is about to make his entrance."

A Marine band played "Hail to the Chief" as the president walked in with the first lady. Everyone stood and applauded. The couple smiled and waved before taking their seats in the front row.

Karen leaned toward Jason. "We should learn from the British," she said. "The prime minister runs the government and leaves the ceremonial duties to the queen. The people have their symbol of state and the prime minister has time to govern."

Jason smiled and nodded in the direction of the first lady. "There's someone who would agree with you," he said. "She would love to escape the spotlight. The media report on what she's wearing and how much she paid for each outfit. She's expected to do good deeds, keep the president happy, and smile even if she has a toothache."

The band swarmed onto the stage in a blaze of satin shirts and flashing guitars. Karen settled back to enjoy the music, but the project was still on her mind. She thought about the section on the Chief of State. Was it really a worthwhile job for a busy Chief Executive?

The answer came unexpectedly during a break in the music. The president stepped onto the stage and picked up a microphone. After a few words of welcome, he said that he had a special award to present. The quiet room grew even more hushed.

An aide stepped forward with a velvet box. The president opened it and held up a gold medal by its red-white-and-blue ribbon. As he did so, a second aide pushed an old man in a wheelchair to the president's side. In a brief ceremony, the president presented the Medal of Freedom to Moses Tilly. Tilly, he said, was a former Olympic athlete who had devoted his life to helping poor children. The applause was loud and prolonged.

Once they reach the White House, America's first ladies are expected to take on a constant round of domestic, social, political, and charitable duties. They work long hours and give up much of their personal privacy. They are paid only in applause and appreciation—if the public approves of what they do. Earning that favorable reaction requires the skills of a diplomat and the toughness of a hockey goalie. Four of the outstanding women who have served as First Lady are as follows:

Martha Washington (1789-1797)
The first president's wife set many precedents for later first ladies. Although she felt like a "state prisoner," she entertained regularly and took on many ceremonial duties. Although she preferred formality, she recognized that a democratic presidency had to be open to everyone.

Abigail Adams (1797-1801)
When she moved into the White House in 1800, the new capital was a muddy wilderness, but the second First Lady dutifully held the proper dinners and receptions. Mrs. Adams had a sharp mind and a ready wit. Like many of the first ladies to follow, she served as the president's unofficial advisor.

Edith Wilson (1915-1921)

Edith Wilson married Woodrow Wilson in 1915. After Wilson was disabled by a stroke in 1919, Mrs. Wilson took over many of the president's routine duties. She insisted that she didn't make major decisions, but some critics charged that she was "running the government." If the stories contain any truth, the United States had a woman as acting president for over a year.

Eleanor Roosevelt (1933-1945)

Any rating of first ladies finds Mrs. Roosevelt at the top of the list. Painfully shy as a girl, she overcame her fears and became a fine public speaker. As first lady she was a gracious hostess, but her real interests lay in the work she did to help the victims of war and poverty. Through her press conferences, lectures, and newspaper column she became the first truly public first lady. Every first lady since then has been given more respect and more public duties because of Mrs. Roosevelt's success.

Jacqueline Kennedy (1961-1963)

The Kennedy Administration will go down in history as a period of nationalism and pride among the American people, and the young and attractive Mrs. Kennedy was as popular as her husband. After finishing the last major renovations on the public rooms of the White House, she invited the public to view the president's home on national television.

"Now I see," Karen thought. "We do need a Chief of State. Only the president can invest a simple ceremony with so much meaning." She remembered the president's visit to a Missouri town after it had been wrecked by a tornado. Who could doubt the nation's concern when its president came in person to express his sympathy?

Jason leaned toward her. "I didn't want to tell you earlier," he said, "but I fixed it with Billings. We'll be taken in to see the president right after the show."

A Visit With The Chief

The president stood up when Karen and Jason were shown into the small sitting room next to the Oval Office. Chet Billings stepped forward to make the introductions.

Karen smiled nervously. After studying his job all week, she would actually be talking to the president! Up close, she saw that he looked tired. He had been working since six o'clock this morning, she realized. Billings had told her that the president read his first briefing papers while still in bed.

What should she say? Everything she had thought of now seemed silly. You can't talk about the weather with the president. But the president knew when to come to the aid of visitors. He waved Karen and Jason to a couch and offered them chocolate chip cookies from a silver tray.

"Chet told me about your project," he said to Karen. "I'm looking forward to reading it. We get so busy around here that sometimes we don't stop to look at what we're doing." His smile broadened. "Tell me, Karen, how would you like to have my job?"

"Mr. President, I hope some day to see a woman in the Oval Office—but it won't be me," she said. "The job is so big! I don't see how you do it."

The president glanced at Billings. "My staff carries much of the load," he said. "Even so, I often feel overwhelmed by all the decisions I'm called on to make. But when I'm feeling down I think about this great country and the trust its people have placed in me. I remember that I have a chance to leave the United States a little better than when I took office. After my term ends, someone else will pick up the burden."

The president turned to Jason and asked about his work at party headquarters. Then he picked up two souvenir pens and handed them to his guests. Each pen was marked with the presidential seal. The gift was the signal that the meeting was over.

As Karen and Jason left, the president was already studying a folder marked TOP SECRET. Was he wearing his Commander-in-Chief's hat now? By this time tomorrow, Karen thought, he'll also have served as Chief Executive, Chief Diplomat, Chief Jurist, Chief Politician, Chief Legislator and Chief of State.

Billings followed the couple into the hallway. "Now that you've finished your interviews," he said to Karen, "I'll expect to see a draft of that visitors' handbook on my desk Monday morning."

Without waiting for an answer, Billings turned and walked back to his office. Karen thought about the amount of work that lay ahead of her. It would be a busy weekend.

She looked at Jason. "Don't the people who work in the White House ever sleep?" she asked.

Glossary

AMBASSADOR. The senior diplomat who is sent to represent a country's interests in a foreign country.

AMNESTY. A pardon granted to an entire group of individuals for offenses committed against the government.

BILL. A proposed law that will be debated and voted on by both the House and Senate.

COMMUTED SENTENCE. A shortened prison term.

DIPLOMATIC RECOGNITION. The establishment of normal relations with another country.

ELECTORAL COLLEGE. The body of electors who vote for the president and the vice president. Six weeks after the general election, the electors gather and cast their ballot for president. Until that time, the outcome of the popular vote is not official.

EMBASSY. The building in a foreign country that houses a country's ambassador and diplomatic staff.

EXECUTIVE AGREEMENT. A presidential agreement with another country that has the force of a treaty.

EXECUTIVE BRANCH. The branch of government that enforces federal law.

EXECUTIVE ORDER. A directive issued by the president that has the force of law.

GERRYMANDER. The practice of dividing a state into legislative districts that favor the party in power.

HEARINGS. Meetings held by a congressional committee for the purpose of gathering information about a bill.

IMPEACHMENT. The legal process which removes a government official from office.

INAUGURATION. The ceremony in which a president is sworn into office at the beginning of the term.

JUDICIAL BRANCH. The branch of government that interprets laws.

LEGISLATIVE BRANCH. Congress, the branch of government that makes the laws.

LOBBY. To try to influence the passage of a bill.

MEDIA. A term referring to the nation's television and radio stations, and its newspapers and magazines.

OVERRIDE. A vote in Congress that passes a bill over the President's veto.

PARDON. The act of freeing a suspected or convicted criminal from further trial or punishment.

PATRONAGE. The power to award government jobs to a political party's supporters.

PENTAGON. The headquarters of the United States Department of Defense.

PORK BARREL PROJECT. A special project voted by Congress that benefits a member's home district.

PROTOCOL. The forms of etiquette and ceremony followed by diplomats and heads of state.

SUMMIT CONFERENCE. A meeting of the heads of state of two or more countries.

TICKET-BALANCING. Choosing candidates whose vote-winning abilities complement each other.

TREATY. A formal agreement between two or more governments.

VETO. The President's power to reject a bill that has been passed by Congress.

WAR POWERS ACT. A law that requires the president to ask approval of any lengthy military action.

Bibliography

Blumberg, Rhoda. *First Ladies*. Franklin Watts, 1981

Couvin, Edward S. *The President; Office and Powers, 1787-1984*. New York University Press, 1984

Fincher, Ernest B. *The Presidency: An American Invention*. Abelard-Schuman, 1977

Johnson, Haynes. *The Working White House*. Praeger Publishers, 1975

Packard, Jerrold M. *American Monarchy: A Social Guide to the Presidency*. Delacorte Press, 1983

Patterson, Bradley H. *The Ring of Power; the White House Staff and Its Expanding Role in Government*. Basic Books, 1988

The White House; an Historic Guide. White House Historical Association, 1982

Index

Adams, John and Abigail, 18

Bush, George, 36, 42, 44, 78

Carter, Jimmy, 36, 67
Commander-In-Chief, *see* the Presidency
Congress
   and budget policy, 21, 26-28
   and defense policy, 44-46
   and foreign policy, 31-36, 38-39
   and judicial appointments, 62-66
   and legislation, 52-58
   and overriding vetoes, 58-59
Constitution, the
   amendment process, 14
   of the presidency, 14-17, 31, 42, 54, 70

Department of Defense, 42, 44, 49-51

Eisenhower, Dwight, 59, 69

Ford, Gerald, 48, 66

Harrison, William, 17

Jackson, Andrew, 67
Jefferson, Thomas, 31
Joint Chiefs of Staff, 49
Johnson, Lyndon, 59, 74

Kennedy, John, 42, 48, 59, 74

McKinley, William, 31

Nixon, Richard, 40, 66, 69, 78
nuclear war, 48

OMB (Office of Management and Budget), 26-28
Oval Office, 10

Pentagon, the, 49
political parties, 70
Presidency, the
   and diplomatic recognition, 40-41
   and executive departments, 22
   and federal appointments, 60-62
   and press conferences, 56-58, 78-79

and summit conferences, 36-40
duties of the president
   as Chief Diplomat, 30-41
   as Chief Executive, 21-29
   as Chief Jurist, 60-69
   as Chief Legislator, 52-59
   as Chief of State, 80-86
   as Chief Politician, 70-79
   as Commander-In-Chief, 42-51
   delegation of, 23
executive agreements, 31-36
executive orders, 53-54
power to pardon, 66-67
requirements for office, 10
role of aides, 28-29
selecting a running mate, 74-78
two-term limit, 10, 14
veto power, 58-59
presidents
   as former generals, 10
   who died in office, 17

Reagan, Ronald, 44, 48, 78
Roosevelt, Franklin, 14, 36, 39-40, 59

State Department, 30, 41
Supreme Court, the, 47, 36, 59, 62, 66, 67

Truman, Harry, 40, 44, 56, 59, 67

Van Buren, Martin, 78
Vetoes, *see* the Presidency
vice presidency
   constitutional duties, 17
   succession to presidency, 14, 17, 78
   term limit, 14

War Powers Act, the, 45-47
Washington, George, 14, 44, 70
White House, the
   family quarters, 18
   first tenants, 18
   office layout, 18
   security, 44, 47-48
   tours, 18
Wilson, Woodrow, 38

Picture Credits